W9-COJ-912

ANCIENT GREECE

Mitchell Lane
PUBLISHERS

P.O. Box 196
Hockessin, Delaware 19707

HOW?D THEY DO THAT?
in...

Ancient Egypt

Ancient Greece

Ancient Mesopotamia

Ancient Rome

The Aztec Empire

Colonial America

Elizabethan England

The Mayan Civilization

The Persian Empire

Pre-Columbian America

ANCIENT
GREECE

RUSSELL ROBERTS

Printing   1   2   3   4   5   6   7   8   9

Library of Congress Cataloging-in-Publication Data
Roberts, Russell, 1953–
   How'd they do that in ancient Greece / by Russell Roberts.
        p. cm.–(How'd they do that)
   Includes bibliographical references and index.
   ISBN 978-1-58415-819-6 (library bound)
   1.   Greece–Civilization–To 146 B.C.–Juvenile literature. I. Title.
   DF77.R54 2010
   938–dc22
                                                                        2009027332

AUTHOR'S NOTE: Roman transliterations of the ancient Greek language will show a *c* for the Greek letter kappa (since Latin had no *k*). Modern Greek scholars use a *k* instead of *c*. Therefore, you may see the same name spelled two ways–for example, *Alcibiades* and *Alkibiades*. In this book, we have used the *k* in most names. However, we have left the common English spellings for names such as Socrates.

PUBLISHER'S NOTE: This story is based on the author's extensive research, which he believes to be accurate. Documentation of his research is on page 60.
   The internet sites referenced herein were active as of the publication date. Due to the fleeting nature of some web sites, we cannot guarantee they will all be active when you are reading this book.

PLB

CONTENTS

I n September 490 BCE (Before the Common Era), ten-year-old Demetrius from Athens was hiding on the plains of Marathon, watching events unfold that could lead to the end of his civilization—and maybe even his life.

Ten days before, Persian general Datis had landed his troops on the plain of Marathon, about 20 miles from the city of Athens, and now the men were preparing for battle. Thousands and thousands of Persians had gathered before their triremes, or three-tiered ships, where they had set up camp on the shore. The soldiers had wanted to punish Athens for aiding a few sister city-states up north that had fallen under Persian rule and then revolted. The rebellious states had pleaded for assistance from their fellow Greeks, but only Athens and Eretria had helped. The Persian army crushed Eretria, and then sailed to Athens to make them pay as well.

Not only did the Persians outnumber the Greeks (modern estimates of the numbers of Persians vary widely, from 20,000 to 60,000), but

ON THE PLAINS OF MARATHON

they had a reputation as fierce fighters. Word of their impending invasion raced through Athens, panicking people and sending shockwaves through the city. How could Athens hope to stop these ferocious warriors? What would happen to everyone if they conquered the city? The men would likely be killed, and the women and children, with no one left to defend them, would be taken away as slaves. Athens would be no more. Some people had already fled in terror, trying to escape what they thought was an inevitable Persian victory.

Many people in Athens wanted the Greek troops to take shelter behind the city's walls and wait for the Persians to come to them, figuring that was their best chance for victory. But Miltiades, the leading *strategos* or general, did not wait to be attacked. Instead, he took an enormous risk and marched his men out to meet the Persians at Marathon.

Demetrius had heard all this talk for days. His parents and their slaves had spoken excitedly about it. As a native-born Greek male,

A modern Greek hoplite reenactor. The shield was critical for the hoplite soldier. By fighting shoulder to shoulder, and holding up his shield, each soldier protected himself and the man next to him.

Demetrius was looking forward to becoming a citizen of Athens—but it would never happen if the Persians won. Wanting to see the battle for himself, he had wrapped a meal of olives and bread in a cloth, then walked the 20 miles to Marathon. It was not unusual for Greek males to walk that far. Physical fitness was a source of pride for them. Wealthy boys started working with a professional trainer at the age of seven.[1] When he had reached Marathon, Demetrius hid in a grove of trees. Now he was waiting, watching the troops on the plain.

Although the Persian army was larger than the Greek army, its infantry was ill-equipped to fight. The average Persian infantryman, or foot soldier, carried a seven-foot-long thrusting spear tipped with an iron spearhead. He dressed in regular clothing, with no armor or helmet. Only wealthy soldiers, mainly cavalrymen, could afford them. Persian armor, called scale armor, was made of small bronze plates sewn to a leather shirt. Exceptionally wealthy soldiers wore iron- or gold-plated armor. The infantrymen relied mainly on their shields for protection. Each elaborately painted shield, called a *spara*, was made of reeds and leather. These were weak compared to the strong bronze shields called *hoplons* carried by the Greek hoplite soldiers. A *hoplon* weighed 12 to 15 pounds.

The hoplites were more heavily armed than most Persian soldiers. They carried thrusting spears measuring six to ten feet in length. Each hoplite also carried a two-foot-long sword, which he used for close fighting. They were well protected in their bronze chest plates, greaves or shin guards, and helmets.

For battle, each army positioned its troops in battle formations. Persian soldiers stood in a row and created a wall with their shields, protecting the cavalry and archers from oncoming hoplites. This formation was called a *sparabara*. As enemy soldiers ran into the Persian formation, they would be met with thousands of glistening spears.

Persian heavy cavalry

Greek soldiers stood in phalanx formations. They worked as a team to defeat their enemy. Each man stood close to his neighbor, holding his shield with his left arm and his spear in his right hand. The phalanx was at least four rows deep and able to advance toward an enemy formation without being penetrated by deadly spears and arrows.

It was the eleventh day since the Persian landing, and the Greek army had decided to attack. Some 25,000 Persians lay in wait as Miltiades led about 11,000 hoplites, mainly from Athens, across the mile-long plain toward them. With a blare of trumpets, the Greeks charged forward to meet the Persians. Amazed by the sheer size of the Persian force, Demetrius wished that Sparta had responded to the Athenians' pleas for help. But Sparta had answered that, for religious reasons, it could not send troops until after the full moon.[2]

Demetrius swelled with pride as the Greeks waded into the Persian ranks, swords swinging. The Greek warriors were fighting bravely, but there were so many Persians . . . just so many.

It is thought that the phalanx formation was invented because it was easy to teach to the Greek soldiers, who were not professionals but citizen-soldiers. However, if everyone did not stay in formation, then the phalanx quickly fell apart.

One of history's most enduring legends comes from the battle of Marathon. According to the tale, a Greek named Pheidippides ran the 20 miles back to Athens with news of the great victory. When he arrived in the city he cried, "Rejoice! We conquer!" then collapsed and died from exhaustion. Now the word marathon is used for any footrace over twenty miles long.

As his heart sank with doubt, he realized that both sides of the Greek formation were advancing ahead of the center. Then, when the center attacked with a rush, the surprised Persians moved to meet them—and the wings on both sides of the Greek formation closed in on them. The Greeks had caught the Persians in a pincers movement and were relentlessly cutting them down. When the battle was over, the Persians had lost over 6,000 men, while Greek casualties numbered just a few hundred.

The Athenians' victory would give Athens the confidence to emerge as a major world power; to become a leader in art, music, and democracy; and to produce a legendary civilization that continues to be studied—something that would not have happened if Persia had been victorious. And Demetrius could grow up to become a citizen of that great city.

The temple of Hephaestus, which overlooks the Agora, is one of the best preserved in modern-day Greece. Hephaestus was the god of fire and of craftsmen. He was especially associated with blacksmiths.

ATHENS, GREATEST OF THE GREEK CITY-STATES

Chapter 1

It is difficult to examine life in ancient Greece because the surviving historical evidence is based almost entirely on the actions and lives of one group of people: the well-to-do adult males who lived in major cities. These were the influential personages in Greek society, so nearly all the information we have deals with their activities. As researcher Robert Garland wrote: "Virtually none of [the surviving historical evidence] focuses on women, adolescents, metics (immigrants), slaves, the disabled, or those living in the countryside."[1]

The period between 500 and 323 BCE is recognized as the Classical Age of Greece.[2] But there wasn't a single country called "Greece," as there is today, and it had no central government. The ancient Greeks lived in *poleis*, which means "city-states." (From the singular *polis* comes the modern word *politics*.) Each city-state was like its own country, and there were hundreds of them, some no larger than a town. No matter how big or small it was, each had its own laws and system of government. The people who lived in ancient Greece did not call themselves Greeks, but "Hellenes."[3]

Of all the city-states, none was greater than Athens. While Athens was a large and bustling city, it was not a city such as we are familiar

with today. For example, there was no organized system of street lighting, even by torches or lanterns. There were no firefighters, and the police force (which was made up of slaves) existed strictly to keep the peace—not to fight crime. There were no hospitals for the sick. Only a few roads were paved.

Athens had three outstanding features. One was a wall that circled the entire city, built to protect its inhabitants from invaders. There were nearly twenty gates in the wall through which people and vehicles could pass.[4] Another feature was a large, flat hilltop called the Acropolis. On it were several temples, including the Parthenon—a magnificent structure dedicated to the goddess Athena.

Athens' third unique feature was a large, rectangular, open piece of ground inside the city known as the Agora. The Agora was the

The Agora was the center of community life in Athens.

heart of Athens, where people from all walks of life met and discussed ideas, talked about the latest news, and gossiped about friends and neighbors. Vendors set up their stands on the Agora and sold fruits, vegetables, and other goods. It was a favorite place of the philosopher Socrates, who taught his followers there. Visitors could watch a group performing a play, or hear a man reciting poetry. Important public buildings, such as the mint and the record office, bordered the Agora.

Politically, Athens was often considered to be the birthplace of democracy because it conceived the "one man–one vote" type of government. But "one man" meant exactly that. In most modern democracies, all citizens—men and women—can vote. Citizenship in ancient Greece was limited to freeborn males over the age of 18 or 21.

No more than 6 to 10 percent of the Greek population were citizens,[5] so although it was "one man, one vote," the governing process was still in the hands of a small group of people. Of 300,000 people living in the city-state of Sparta, it is estimated that only 4,000 were citizens.[6]

People today use money in the form of paper bills and coins to buy things. In ancient Greece, a person could use coins mainly to trade with other cities that also issued coins. Most of the coins bore pictures that made them immediately identifiable as being from a particular city-state. Coins from Athens were imprinted with an owl, which was the symbol of the goddess Athena—Athens' primary god and chief protector—and signified wisdom. But in cities where trade was not as important, the use of coins seemed unnecessary. Sparta, for example, used an unconventional system of currency requiring iron bars.[7]

Athenian coins featuring the sea go[d] Poseidon (left), a s[ea] turtle, Athena (top right), and an owl.

People in Athens were either rich or poor. There was no middle class as exists in many countries today. In the United States, every citizen is required to pay taxes. In Athens, however, only the wealthy citizens paid taxes.

Although Athens did not have a police force as we know it, any victim of a crime could arrest the criminal and bring him before a magistrate (judge). If the person was unable to make the arrest, then a magistrate could make the arrest for him. According to Athenian law, anyone could request legal action. The plaintiff (the one with the complaint) and the defendant had a hearing called an *anakrisis* before a magistrate. At the hearing, the plaintiff swore his charges were true, and the defendant had to either admit guilt or plead innocent.[8] Then a trial date was set.

Modern people are used to trials sometimes lasting for months. Trials in Athens lasted just one day. Juries were made up of citizens over thirty years old. There were often many jurors, because it was felt that the bigger the jury, the harder it would be to bribe the members.[9]

If the defendant was found guilty, his punishment never included imprisonment, as is common today. A fine, exile, or some loss of citizenship rights was the likely sentence. People who committed harsher crimes, such as murder, were executed. Some crimes were considered so serious that after execution the criminal's body was not buried but

The River Styx separated the world of the living from the world of the dead. The river supposedly wound around Hades (also known as the Underworld) nine times. Its water was so foul that if a god drank from it, the deity would lose his or her voice for nine years.

was tossed into a rocky pit called the *barathron*, where it was left to rot. By denying burial, the Greeks were condemning the dead person to walk up and down the banks of the River Styx forever, never to be granted entrance to Hades—the Underworld of the spirits.

The Execution of Socrates

In 399 BCE, Athenians tried and executed the philosopher Socrates in one of the most famous cases of its kind in history. To us today, it seems incredible that a man who is still known as a profound thinker was found guilty and executed by a society that prided itself on the enlightenment of its citizens. Why was Socrates tried in the first place, and why was he executed?

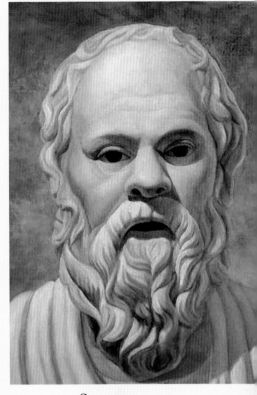

Socrates

While we think of Socrates as a wise man and great thinker, ordinary Athenians did not view him that way. Socrates was not a supporter of democracy as practiced in Athens. He did not believe that Athenians were capable of governing themselves through democracy, but rather needed to be governed by a strong leader.

Two of Socrates' former pupils—Alkibiades and Kritias—were responsible for temporarily overthrowing Athenian democracy twice between 411 and 403 BCE. In particular, because Kritias killed so many Athenian democrats, a lot of people probably saw Socrates as a dangerous man whose words and teachings produced murderous tyrants.

Another anti-democratic uprising in 401 BCE further inflamed Athenians toward Socrates. They believed he was corrupting his young students against Athenian ideas, and the clamor to punish the philosopher grew. Socrates was brought to trial two years later.

The trial of Socrates took nine or ten hours, all in one day. There were 500 jurors present. No accounts of the trial exist except those written by two of Socrates' students—Plato and Xenophon. Historians suspect that the accounts of both have been colored by the two to make Socrates look good.

For his defense, Socrates gave a long speech that was not apologetic, and indicated that he would go on doing what he was doing: encouraging youths to think about morals, and preaching against democracy, the very backbone of Athenian life. After he was found guilty, and the sentence was to be determined, Socrates seemed to mock the entire trial by asking to be rewarded rather than punished. At that point, 80 jury members who had initially found him innocent voted for his execution. Socrates was sentenced to drink poisonous hemlock.

Greek women spent much of their lives indoors. The only time they were permitted to leave their homes without the accompaniment of their husbands was during the various festivals of Dionysus.

WOMEN IN GREEK SOCIETY

Chapter 2

The Greeks lived in households, much like modern households, called *oikoi*.[1] However, in Greece, the *oikos* included everyone and everything that was together under one roof, including servants, slaves, livestock, and any other property. The head of the *oikos* was the oldest male.

While Greek men were seen as important to society, the women were not. A Greek woman was to be seen but not heard. She had few rights and few privileges. Her main duty was that of producing children, and for that she needed to get married as soon as possible.

From the scant evidence available, it seems that females in their early to mid teens married men who were in their twenties and thirties.[2] The great philosopher Plato argued that men were ready to be married by age thirty,[3] implying that they were traditionally much younger than this on their wedding day.

Typically, marriages were arranged, so females married whoever was chosen for them. Rather than love, marriages were usually determined by wealth and status: An Athenian male would select a bride not based on affection, but according to how much wealth or power she could bring him. Because of the lack of business or industry, there were few other opportunities to make money and become wealthy. A system of arranged marriages was logical—although hardly romantic.

Because of the age differences between the man and woman getting married, the emotional toll of marriage on the female must have been enormous. She had to literally go from being a child one day to becoming a man's wife the next. Not only was she removed from her family, but as a wife, she suddenly had to run a household. Although she must have known marriage would come early for her, it must have been a lonely, frightening time for a young girl.

There is a famous Greek myth that is a metaphor for this situation. According to the story, Persephone, daughter of Demeter, the goddess of the harvest, was frolicking on the earth when the god Hades charged up from his gloomy underworld kingdom and snatched her away to make her his bride. Demeter was so sad over the loss of her daughter that she allowed the earth to grow cold and barren. A compromise by Zeus (king of the gods) allowed Persephone to spend six months with Demeter and six months with Hades each year.

On its surface, this myth is an explanation of why the earth has different seasons. Yet it can also be seen as an example of Greek marriages—a young girl torn from her family by an older man.

Athenian weddings were much different than modern weddings. On her wedding day, an Athenian bride took a bath with water poured from a special vase. This was followed by a feast at the home of her father. There she sat with a veil on, apart from everyone else. Small cakes covered with sesame seeds were served at the feast. It was thought that these cakes helped make the woman fertile—again, the idea was that she should produce children as soon as possible. After that the groom brought the bride, still veiled, to her new home. Once there she finally removed her veil, and the couple was expected to start a family right away.

There was tremendous pressure on a wife to have children. Her husband and his family all wanted her to produce a male child as soon as possible. Greek society in general expected a woman of child-bearing years to have as many children as she could. The odds of a child dying were great, infant mortality rates were high, and the population was

Hades Abducts
Persephone, *by*
G.L. Bernini,
Villa Borghese

constantly being whittled down by war, disease, and other causes.[4]

However, pregnancy and childbirth were risky for women. Miscarriages and death during labor were common, and because of poor hygiene, the risk of infection was always present. Births took place at home, usually with the help of a midwife—a woman who had experience delivering babies. A doctor was called only if a woman's life was in danger.

In modern society, science and medicine have made great advances, so we sometimes tend to dismiss cultures of long ago as primitive and lacking in any medical knowledge. But the ancient Greeks were very accurate in some of their medical advice—and some of it could even be applied today. For example, Plato thought that a pregnant woman should perform gymnastics—in effect, exercise—to improve the health of both herself and her baby. Aristotle, a scientist and philosopher, recommended that a pregnant woman avoid salt and alcohol, and take a daily walk.[5] These tips have been proven to be sound advice.

Plato

In other respects, the lack of knowledge—and the wealth of misinformation—was shocking indeed. Aristotle thought women were actually unsuccessful men.[6] He thought that a female's lack of activity made her more "formless," and thus unable to be a man. As he saw it, men

Aristotle

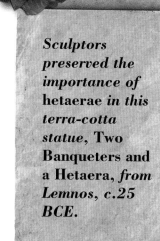

Sculptors preserved the importance of hetaerae *in this* **terra-cotta statue,** **Two Banqueters and a Hetaera,** *from* **Lemnos, c.25 BCE.**

were a step above women on the evolutionary scale. Women, he believed, were on their way to deformity.

It is speculated that Greek homes were so plain and unassuming because the man spent little time there[7] (find out more about these homes in Chapter Five). He preferred instead to walk to the marketplace or to the public baths and converse with his friends, or go to the gymnasium for exercise. A Greek wife was almost strictly confined to the home (The exception is the woman from Sparta, who was encouraged to exercise outside to keep fit.[8]). There she supervised the children, as well as the rest of the household, including the slaves. She was also expected to be capable on the loom, as all clothing was made at home.

There were three classes of women in ancient Greek society. The first consisted of women who were married, and the second class was made up of prostitutes. The third, called the *hetaerae,* served as not

only physical, but also intellectual and social partners to men. Unlike prostitutes, these women sometimes formed one-on-one relationships with the men they accompanied. They were able to move freely through society and attended social places such as the market and the theater. *Hetaerae* were usually foreign women who possessed such skills as dancing, playing music, and singing.

Ironically, given their low social status, women were eligible for one very important role in ancient Greece: priestess. From the age of seven on, girls from prominent families would be involved in a series of sacred rituals.[9] A girl could start out as a participant in festivals, and work her way up to maintaining a god's statue in a temple. So that they could do this well, girls were taught woodworking.[10]

One of the most revered priestesses was the Pythia at Delphi. The Greeks believed she spoke for Apollo, the god of the sun, light, and music.

Slavery in
Ancient Athens

In Athens, slavery was an accepted part of society. The Greek attitude toward slavery was that it was not so good to be a slave, but it was good to have one.[11] Slaves were not allowed to vote, but they could own other slaves.

Athens likely had more slaves than most of the other Greek city-states. One estimate is that affluent Athenians owned two or three slaves, and the wealthy owned upwards of twenty.[12] Some people owned more than that: The wealthy Athenian Nikias owned 1,000 slaves.[13] He had so many that he rented them out to others. Sparta had about 9,000 citizens who controlled about 100,000 slaves, or helots, as they were called.

Domestic slaves did every job imaginable: washing, cooking, nursing, teaching, cleaning, and building. The

A slave market. Debtors or prisoners of war could be sold as slaves.

slaves could be and were treated cruelly sometimes, although there were laws protecting them from violence. If a slave ran away and was recaptured, he or she could be branded with a hot iron. It was virtually impossible for a slave to lodge a legal complaint against his or her master, and even then the cards were stacked against the slave. In court, a slave's testimony could be accepted only if the slave had been tortured!

Yet as cruelly as slaves could be treated, there were also attempts to be kind to them. For example, when a slave became a member of a household in Athens, he or she underwent a ceremony similar to how a bride was welcomed into her new home. Nuts and fruits were offered as a symbol of good health and prosperity. This was done so that the slave would be protected by the goddess of the hearth, Hestia. Greek literature contains scenes of slaves and masters enjoying one another's company, rather than portraying a contentious relationship. Indeed, some slaves grew so close to their families that they were buried in the family's grave plots.

The opposite of such kindness and devotion was found in the silver mines southeast of Athens. The slaves who labored in these mines endured harsh conditions. The work went on 24 hours a day, in shifts that were ten hours long.

Artemis was a major goddess for the ancient Greeks. Besides childbirth and virginity, she was also the goddess of the forests and the hunt. The twin sister of Apollo, Artemis was often shown carrying a bow and arrow.

CHiLDReN AND THe eLDeRLY

Chapter 3

The birth of a child today is usually celebrated by family and friends. Sometimes, it is even announced to friends and neighbors with colorful signs or giant figures of storks on the front lawn. But in ancient Athens, births were handled quite differently. The virgin goddess Artemis was prominent in the ceremonies that accompanied the birth of the baby. It seems that the Athenians tried to soothe the goddess's anger over the woman's disobedience to her by offering prayers to her before the birth, and later by bringing clothes to her shrine as an offering.[1] Instead of joyously celebrating the birth, the Greeks coated the walls of the home with pitch, perhaps to block any indication of the birth from getting out to the community.[2] The only notification of the new child's arrival was the hanging of either an olive branch (for a boy) or a piece of wool (for a girl) on the front door.

The new child was introduced to the rest of the household five days after its birth. This allowed the baby to come under the protection of the household gods. Instead of a baptism or similar ceremony, the father would run around the hearth while holding the infant. This was supposed to place the baby under the care of Hestia. Just as happens today, relatives brought gifts for the newborn.

If the baby was a boy and in good health, then the child could look forward to a good life. However, if the infant was sickly, the father might abandon it by placing it outside where it would be exposed to the elements. This was done in order not to kill the baby outright, but to leave it up to the Moirae, the three goddesses of fate: Clotho, Lachesis, and Atropos. They would decide whether the child would live or die.

In Sparta, parents didn't have a choice whether to care for a sickly child or not. There, government officials examined every male baby born.[3] Those who were strong enough to be raised as warriors were allowed to live. The rest were left outside to die. There are no written accounts of female babies

Ancient Greek potty trainer

A Sick Child Brought into the Temple of Aesculapius, *John William Waterhouse, 1877. Greeks often sought the help of the gods in curing illnesses by praying to them and offering them gifts.*

being examined for fitness, but it is possible that they were. Spartans wanted women to be good child-bearers.

Even if they were healthy, though, female infants ran a much greater risk of being abandoned than males. Not only were women less valued than men in Greek society, but families had to supply daughters with expensive dowries in order to attract a man and get married. Thus, for a family to have more than two daughters was rare.[4]

When a child in Athens was four years old, he or she was brought to the Anthesteria, or Flower Festival. There, the child was given a wreath to wear as a crown, and a small jug called a *khous.* This festival was an important moment in a child's life, a rite of passage; it was the first time he drank wine—a gift from the god Dionysus. Children who died before attending their first Anthesteria were buried with a *khous,* perhaps to enable them to have in death what they could not in life.

Since the dawn of time, children have played with toys, and Athenian children were no exception. Among their toys were horses on wheels, boats, rattles, and dolls with arms

Festivals in ancient Greece were usually held in honor of a god or goddess, with great pageantry.

Knucklebones could be made of the original animal bones, or they could be fashioned from glass.

and legs that moved. Game balls were made by blowing up a pig's bladder and then heating it in the ashes of the fire to make it rounder. In a game called knucklebones, kids threw the knucklebones (the ankle joints of a cloven-hooved animal) up in the air and attempted to catch them on the back of their hand before they hit the ground.

Initially, schooling in Athens was done by private tutors. Often, whether a child went to school or not depended upon his family's financial situation. Most boys began school around the age of seven. Later, during the Hellenistic Period (the time between the death of Alexander the Great in 323 BCE and the death of Cleopatra VII in 30 BCE), a public education system was established in Greece.

Boys in Athens studied only reading, writing, music, and physical education. The students used a sharp, pointed object to scratch their letters onto a waxed wooden tablet. Pupils were also required to memorize large portions of famous poems and songs. At festivals and other events, prizes were given out for recitation.

Girls received almost no formal education. It was thought that educating a female was "spoiling" her for marriage. A girl received domestic

education from her mother. She would learn how to run a household and do other things that were expected of good wives.

It is unclear to what age the ancient Greeks generally lived, for their tombstones did not list a year of birth and a year of death, as is the common practice today. Only when the person had lived to a ripe old age and was proud of the achievement would the age be listed.

By the same token, it is unclear if the concept of retirement was something that the Greeks followed when they got older. Today people work for years and look forward to retirement. But the modern idea of having elderly people live in a nursing home or similar facility was unknown to the Greeks. They considered the care of the elderly to be a sacred honor to be carried out by their children. Greek law carried penalties for those who did not take care of their elderly parents. An Athenian who ignored his duty was fined and partially stripped of his rights as a citizen. The elderly likely worked around the household or made themselves useful somehow, unless an illness made that impossible.

Since medicine was still in its infancy, there was little a physician could do to help ease the suffering of the elderly if they got sick. An older person who became critically ill almost certainly had to suffer with their sickness. Hippocrates, known as the Father of Medicine, experimented with natural cures, and some of them successfully relieved pain. Most people,

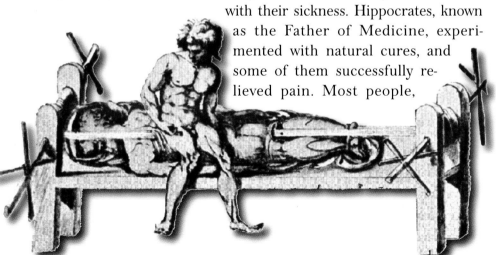

Hippocrates' invention, the Hippocratic Bench, was a forerunner of the traction devices used in modern orthopedics.

Asklepios was the god of medicine and healing. His mother died giving birth to him, but his father rescued him from her womb. He was thought to be such a skilled healer that he was able to bring the dead back to life.

however, believed illness was caused by the gods' displeasure, so they sought relief in the temples of Asklepios, the god of medicine.

Asklepios and his daughters, Hygeia and Panacea, were the protectors of good health. The Greeks believed that in order for a sick person to be healed, he or she had to have a vision of Asklepios and his daughters. If the person was visited by them in a dream, then he or she would supposedly be healed. In addition, people would hang stone carvings of their afflicted body parts in trees outside the temple, hoping that their prayers would be carried on the wind to Asklepios.

A Boy in Sparta

If ancient Athens is remembered for democracy and culture, Sparta is remembered for its militaristic society. A male in Sparta essentially had his life mapped out for him from early childhood until he was sixty years old.

Sparta did not recognize the family as the main unit of society, as did Athens. Instead, Sparta subordinated the family to the *agoge*, a system of military training that dominated a male's life. This began at birth, when infants were bathed with wine instead of water, in the belief that this toughened them.[5]

A boy first entered the *agoge* when he was seven years old. He was trained in such

Education in Sparta

subjects as endurance, athletics, and creative thinking. The object was to turn the boy—whether he wanted to be or not—into the perfect citizen-soldier.

Life for these boys was difficult. They went barefoot to toughen their feet, played naked, slept on hard beds, and were taught to endure as much pain as possible. According to a famous story, a boy once stole a fox, intending to eat it, when he saw a group of Spartan soldiers approaching. Not wanting to be caught stealing, the boy hid the fox under his shirt. He then allowed the fox to eat into his stomach, without showing any pain, rather than admit to the soldiers that he had stolen it.

At age eighteen, a Spartan boy became a military cadet, and at age twenty he joined the state militia. Between the ages of twenty and thirty, he could marry, but he had to still live and eat with his fellow soldiers. The primary meal of Spartan soldiers was called black broth—pork cooked in blood and seasoned with salt and vinegar.[6] The soldier then served in the military until he reached sixty years old. At age sixty (if he lived that long), a Spartan male was finally allowed to return home and live with his family.

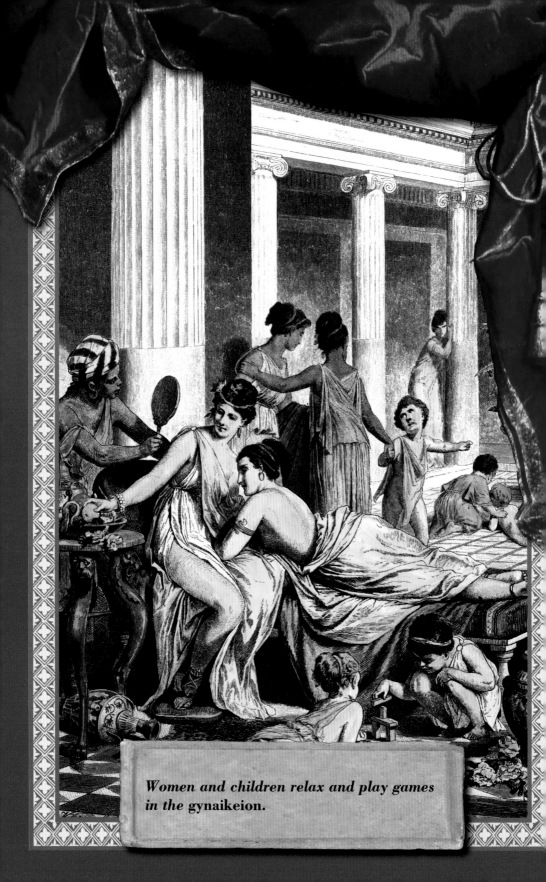

Women and children relax and play games in the gynaikeion.

In some respects, ancient Athens was a city of contrasts. For example, although it boasted magnificent temples and public buildings that were built using the finest craftsmanship, its private homes were bland, ordinary, and cheaply constructed.[1]

Today, most homes are built of wood. But in Greece, wood was both scarce and expensive, so it houses were usually built with stones, which were simply placed one on top of another. Mud, either baked or unbaked, was used to fill in the cracks and keep the elements out. These walls were very thin. Thieves could break in by merely knocking a hole in the wall. They could either reach in and take what they wanted, or make the hole large enough to crawl through. As might be expected, burglary was common.

Inside, the walls were covered with plaster. Sometimes they were painted, but apparently painters were hard to come by in Athens. According to Plutarch, the politician Alkibiades once locked a painter inside his house for three months until he finished the job.[2]

Floors in the homes were earthen. Sometimes they were covered with animal skins or reed mats. Windows were small, really just holes, and placed high in the wall close to the ceiling. In winter the windows were covered with boards or cloth. If a household could afford them, wooden shutters were also used on windows for extra protection from the elements. Wood was considered so precious that when Athenians who lived outside the city moved inside the walls for protection, they brought their wooden doors and shutters with them.

It was a matter of honor to Greek men that their wives not be seen by the public when at home. It was considered an outrageous act for a person to enter a home where women might be present, unless specifically invited to do so by the master of the house.[3] Thus houses had a *gynaikeion* in the rear, which was a living area specifically for women. Men also had their own separate area, called an *andron,* where dinner and drinking parties, called symposia, took place. Privacy within the household was not a concern, so there were no hallways. People had to pass through one room to reach another.[4]

Today, lights in homes are electrical, and we have illumination at the flick of a switch. But electricity was centuries away from being discovered, so the Greeks had to use other sources of light. One of the most common was a type of lamp that used a wick floating in olive oil. Several were needed to light a room.

Greek homes were not extensively furnished. One of the most common items was a *kline,* which served as both a bed and couch. Its seat consisted of intertwined rope cords. If an elderly man lived in the

An oil lamp

home, he sat on a special chair called a *thronos.*[5] A small, low table with three legs was placed before each *kline.* On these were placed food and drink for the males, who ate "reclining" on the couch. (Women ate sitting upright, much like we do today.)

Greek wine jar

Bread was a staple of the Greek diet. It was eaten with honey, olive oil, or cheese. Meat was often served at festivals, as an offering to the gods, so it was rarely eaten at home. The typical Greek diet also contained fish, such as mackerel, tuna, sardines, and eels. Common fruits and vegetables were cabbage, carrots, olives, figs, apples, and pears. Olives and olive oil were prominently used by the Greeks. In a myth that explains why Athena was chosen over Poseidon to be the patron deity of Attica, Athena wins a contest when she gives the city an olive tree.

Wine was the overwhelming drink of choice for the Greeks. Milk was used primarily for cooking, and beer was considered a drink for lesser people. Again, the importance of how the Greeks felt about wine can be found in a story. In the *Odyssey* by Homer, Odysseus and his men are trapped in the cave of the cyclops Polyphemus. Polyphemus is described as drinking goat's milk—truly the mark of a savage creature. Odysseus' men escape after Polyphemus drinks his fill of the men's wine.

For the Athenians to get water, they had to bring it from outside the home, often from a well in the yard. Either the mistress of the house or, more likely, slaves had to bring jugs over to the well, fill them, and carry them back into

Greek clothing did not follow any particular fashion or style, but was worn for comfort. Clothes were made at home. It was a woman's job to make sure that her family had enough clothes. If they did not, either she or a slave made the garments.

the house. Some people used containers to catch rainwater as it ran off the roof.

In Athens, every article of clothing was made at home. There were no latest fashions or trends to follow. Clothing was made for ease and comfort. Initially, women wore a heavy woolen garment called a *peplos,* which was virtually shapeless. It had a belt at the waist and was attached at the shoulders by two long pins. However, according to legend, the *peplos* was replaced because when a solitary soldier returned from a battle, he was stabbed to death by women using the pins. (They were both outraged that he alone had escaped, and were frantic to find out what had happened to their husbands in the fight.)[6] Thereafter the *chiton,* a garment made of linen that used much shorter pins and was a bit more flattering to the female form, replaced the *peplos.* Women also wore earrings, rings, necklaces and other types of jewelry to enhance their appearance. Today the trend is to promote natural fragrances for perfume, using ingredients from plants instead of

chemicals, and that's how the Greeks made their perfume as well: by boiling the petals of flowers.

The ancient Greeks believed that the paler and whiter a woman's skin, the more beautiful she was. Some women used makeup to make their skin look whiter. The fact that women stayed indoors so much also contributed to their pallid look.

For formal occasions, men wore a *chiton.* For casual affairs, the typical male wore an *exomis,* a short tunic that ended above the knee. A loincloth served as an undergarment—when men wore undergarments.

Both men and women wore sandals. When walking a long way, they wore short boots instead. Women who wanted to wear shoes more stylish than sandals wore ones with platform heels. However, in the home, people usually went barefoot.

Wealthy males often sported beards or mustaches. Their hair was worn long, but the style grew shorter as their civilization flourished. Athenian females usually put their hair up in a variety of styles, and wore it down only for

Myrtle was used to make perfume. The plant was considered sacred to the goddesses Aphrodite and Demeter.

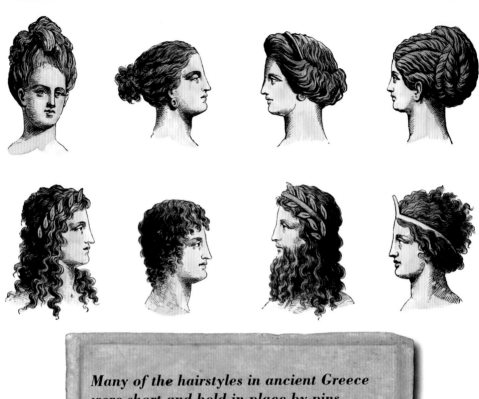

Many of the hairstyles in ancient Greece were short and held in place by pins, combs, and bands. Bangs and ponytails were nonexistent.

special occasions, such as for festivals. Slaves were usually clean-shaven.

Ironically, it was the warrior Spartans who lavished great attention on their hair.[7] They wore it long and took care to keep it combed, gleaming, and shiny—not exactly the type of appearance that is common in today's military! Their long braids were meant to taunt the enemy. It was a dare to see just how close the enemy could get to a Spartan before he was defeated. The answer was usually: not close enough to pull his braid!

The Symposium

While Greek homes were usually drab, there was one occasion at which the Greeks spruced up the house and let themselves go—the dinner party, or symposium.

Before the party, the host would list the names of the guests—male only—on a wax tablet, along with the day and hour of the event. A slave would take the tablet to the various guests' houses.

The home was fixed up for the occasion. Walls were decorated with flowers and ivy or vine streamers. The guests wore garlands and reclined on couches in the *andron*—one of the main rooms of the house primarily used for such parties. Scattered around near the couches were three-legged tables loaded with food and drink.

After the food was eaten and the tables taken away, the real party started. After-dinner events could range from the serious and solemn—Plato told of one symposium in which several long speeches were given on the nature of love—to amusing. The Greek writer Xenophon told of one party that started with the arrival of a professional comedian. His performance was followed by two girls and a boy who played musical instruments and danced. Then a female performer set up a large circular object with swords sticking out of it. She turned somersaults into and out of the circle, to the amazement of all, who wondered how she could do this and not get impaled.

Sometimes the dinner party entertainment was much less polished, such as when songs were sung or poetry recited. The selections could be either traditional or made up on the spot. A favorite game at this time was called *kottabos.* Each person dipped his fingers in the remnants of wine in his cup. He then flicked the wine droplets at a target, such as a disk balanced on a stand. The object was to knock the disk down. The winner was not only the person who knocked over the disk, but also the one who threw his wine with the most style.

A Greek symposium

Zeus was the king of the gods. He was handsome, vain, boastful, and fearless. When angry or in battle, he hurled thunderbolts. He also liked women—both mortal and immortal—and had many children.

The Greek male seemed to like nothing more than meeting others on the street, talking and conversing with them. Thus, although he was out of the house a lot, a Greek did not technically need a place to go in order to "go out."

One place the ancient Greeks did go was a god's temple, to pray for his or her help or to present an offering to the god. Just like many modern people, the Greeks were religious—but their religious outlook was very different. Many religions today preach that there is only one God; the ancient Greeks believed in many gods. They also believed that upon death, a person's inner spirit, or *psyche,* left the body and traveled to the Underworld. Once there, the *psyche* would be sent to one of three locations. The virtuous and heroic spirits spent eternity in Elysium, a paradise. Those who were damned were sent to Tartarus, or hell. The rest resided in Hades, the overall gloomy, dark part of the Underworld that was neither heaven nor hell. There was no special creed associated with Greek religion, and no specific book, such as the Bible or Koran, that contained the teachings of the religion.

The Colossus of Rhodes was a huge bronze statue of the Greek sun god Helios, erected about 280 BCE to guard the entrance to the harbor at Rhodes.

The Greeks thought that the gods were everywhere and in everything—the rocks, trees, water—everywhere! There was a specific god for weather, one for crops, one for war, etc. The interaction between Greeks and their gods was a two-way street. The gods wanted to be remembered and honored by humans, so were happy when a person respected them. Humans, on the other hand, either wanted the gods to grant them something, or worried about what the gods would do to them if they were angered.[1]

Since the gods were everywhere and in all things, the Greeks figured it was best to keep them happy.[2] This was accomplished through prayer, sacrifice, and perhaps gifts. The gifts could be as simple as jugs of fine

A statue of Aphrodite, the Greek goddess of love and beauty, at the British Museum. Aphrodite married Hephaestus, the god of fire.

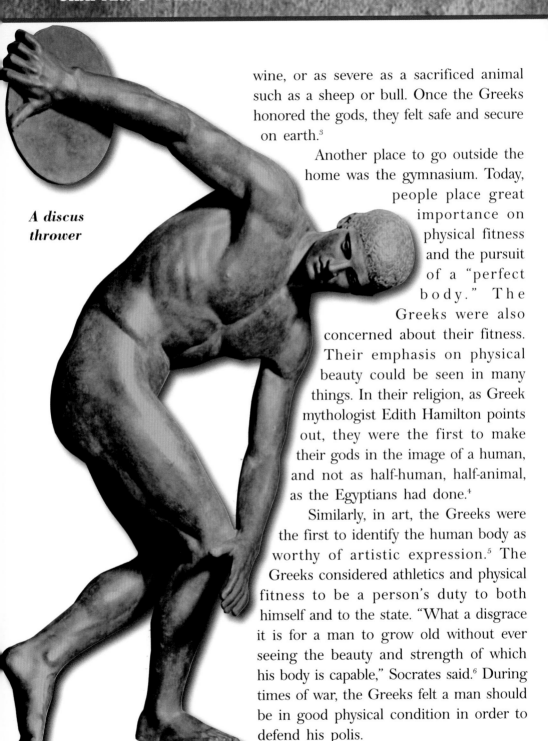

A discus thrower

wine, or as severe as a sacrificed animal such as a sheep or bull. Once the Greeks honored the gods, they felt safe and secure on earth.[3]

Another place to go outside the home was the gymnasium. Today, people place great importance on physical fitness and the pursuit of a "perfect body." The Greeks were also concerned about their fitness. Their emphasis on physical beauty could be seen in many things. In their religion, as Greek mythologist Edith Hamilton points out, they were the first to make their gods in the image of a human, and not as half-human, half-animal, as the Egyptians had done.[4]

Similarly, in art, the Greeks were the first to identify the human body as worthy of artistic expression.[5] The Greeks considered athletics and physical fitness to be a person's duty to both himself and to the state. "What a disgrace it is for a man to grow old without ever seeing the beauty and strength of which his body is capable," Socrates said.[6] During times of war, the Greeks felt a man should be in good physical condition in order to defend his polis.

Javelin throwing prepared peltasts (light infantry) for battle.

The gymnasium served as both an exercise facility and social gathering place. These were not gyms we are familiar with today; they were located outdoors. At the gymnasium, men threw javelins, tossed the discus, and also ran. Gymnasiums were usually located near a river, where the participants could bathe after exercising. Men would socialize during their exercise session, and also later on, perhaps while sitting under a shady tree after bathing.

Greeks often went to theatrical performances. Plays reached a level of unequaled importance when they were included in the Great Dionysia (or City Dionysia), a four-day festival in honor of the god Dionysus. Before the plays started, a statue of the god was carried into the theater, so Dionysus himself could watch the performance.

The plays in the Great Dionysia were primarily tragedies, although some comedies were permitted. Once the plays to be performed were selected, the work to put them on began. According to one estimate, it took 1,500 people to put on the plays at the Great Dionysia.[7]

It is estimated that more than 15,000 people attended these performances. From the slopes of the Acropolis, they watched at least four plays performed each day—more if a comedy was included.[8] The audience was expected to sit for about ten hours total. The only breaks came in the gaps between plays. (Could you sit still that long?)

Besides the Great Dionysia, the Athenians attended many festivals. There were at least sixty festivals per year, and there were many more local ones held as well. Festivals were a combination of religious and social occasions. Typical activities included feasting, religious observances, athletic contests, and dramatic or musical competitions.

Going to a theater or festival was usually a local trip for the Greeks, but when they had to travel long distances, they either walked or went

The Odeon of Herodes Atticus, a stone theater on the south slope of the Acropolis, could hold 5,000 people. Herodes Atticus built the theater to honor his wife, Aspasia.

by sea. Only the very rich had horses. Chariots and other vehicles with wheels were used only for short distances. Whereas today there is a network of hotels, motels, and inns for travelers, the Greeks developed a system known as *xenia*, which means "guest-friendship." Under *xenia*, an aristocrat who was traveling was offered room and board by another aristocrat. Later he would be expected to return the favor.

Today, millions of people leave the house to go to work in an office or store, for example, but this was not the case in ancient Greece. Many Athenians were small farmers. (Greek law prevented anyone from owning too much land.) Estimates are that 9 out of 10 citizens of a city-state were farmers.[9] They raised animals for meat and milk, and typically grew olives, grapes, and grains such as barley. But they did not grow crops

Many Greek farmers planted their crops on rocky soil near the mountains.

with the idea of selling them. The roads were too primitive, and it was too expensive to send material over them, to make that idea practical.

A small part of the population worked in manufacturing, but these were little enterprises, and nothing like the manufacturing plants of today. For instance, it is estimated that over the course of 100 years, Athens—which was famous for the pottery it produced—had just 500 people working in the pottery industry, and most of them worked in groups of six.[10]

Today, retail stores not only offer a variety of merchandise to purchase, but they also provide job opportunities. However, the stalls and stands that were set up in Athens to sell things were only temporary, and were usually staffed by just the person who produced the goods to sell there. There were no stores as we know them.

The ancient Greeks considered the idea of working for someone else as worse than working as a slave.[11] The best situation for someone who wanted to work was to be an employee of the state, because then the worker was not answerable to just one person.

The Gods on Earth

Two of the most famous Greek myths involve Zeus, traveling, and the great flood. Not only do they illustrate how the Greeks explained things by telling stories about the gods, but they also show how the gods sometimes directly interacted with humans. The stories also demonstrate the lack of any organized system of facilities for the traveler, and how a traveler in those days depended upon the kindness of others.

The first story involves Zeus, who wanted to know that people were honoring the gods. He decided to visit the country of Phrygia (part of modern-day Turkey) along with his son Hermes. Disguised as human travelers, they wandered about Phrygia until they came to a city. The gods started knocking at the doors of some very nice houses. When a door was opened, Zeus explained that he and Hermes were travelers who were hungry and tired. They needed food and rest. At each house, the door was slammed in their faces, and no welcome was given.

When the gods knocked at the door of a small cabin, an old woman named Baucis and her husband, Philemon, welcomed the gods inside and gave them food and drink. Their reward was to be spared—for Zeus flooded the city because the people there were so uncaring.

In the second story, Zeus came to earth because he had heard that mankind was growing cruel. He

Zeus on his throne

disguised himself as a traveler and went to a castle. There he identified himself as a god, and asked for the respect that any god, as well as any traveler, should receive. The owner of the house—named Lykaon—laughed at him, and Zeus suspected that Lykaon planned to kill him. Zeus then revealed himself as a god. Lykaon realized his mistake and ran away, but Zeus turned him into a wolf. Deciding that humanity had become vicious and unfeeling, the king of the gods sent a great flood to wipe out all people so that humanity could start anew.

MAKE YOUR OWN HOPLITE SHIELD

With a little ingenuity, you can build a shield fit for battle (or at least display or Halloween!). Here's how:

Materials you will need:
A pizza box (or 2 pieces of cardboard about the same size)
Wide masking tape or duct tape
Scissors
Stapler
Paints (tempera or watercolor) and paintbrush

Here is what to do:
1. Cut the lid and bottom off the pizza box so that you have two large pieces of the same size. Draw a large circle on one and cut it out. You may like to draw 2 "bite" shapes on 2 sides of the circle to make a pear-shaped shield like the black one in the photo above. Cut out your shape following the lines you've drawn.

2. Cut a straight line from the side of this shape right to the center and stop. Place your hands on opposite sides of this cut and gently pull the shape inward onto itself, making the center cone out slightly (about 5 inches). Staple the overlapping edges together, and cover the seam with tape. This is the shield's top.

3. Trace the outside of the cone shape you just made onto the second piece of cardboard. Next, draw a circle about 4 inches wide inside the first circle. Cut out the circle. You now have a ring that matches the size of the bottom of the cone.

4. Tape the cone and the ring together by taping around the edge.

5. Cut one or two 12-inch strips, about one and a half inches wide, from the sides of the pizza box. Tape or staple these "handles" inside the shield, like the handles shown above.

6. Be sure to paint a solid color and a 2-3 inch border color on your shield, then paint a face, symbol, or design over the wide center. You can paint the inside a solid color. Now you're ready to march!

ADRIATIC

SEA

Paleste

MACEDONI

Pella

EPIRUS

MT.
OLYMPUS

CORCYRA

THESSALY

Cynoscephalae
Pharsalus

Actium

AETOLIA

Thermopylae

Delphi

CEPHAIONIA

Patroe

ACHAEA

ARCADIA

Mantinea

PELOPONNES

Messene

IONIAN SEA

MESSENIA

Sparta

Sphacteria

LACC

Where in the World?

TIMELINE

BCE

1250	Trojan War (according to Herodotus)
508	Kleisthenes begins reforming the Athenian code of laws, and establishes a democratic constitution
494	Ionian revolt against the Persians is defeated
490	Athens defeats Persia at the Battle of Marathon
483	Silver mines discovered near Athens; Athens begins building its naval fleet, which will eventually help them rule the Greek world
477	Athens leads Delian league, a group of poleis working together for trade and defense
461–445	First Peloponnesian War is fought between Spartans and the Delian League.
460–429	Perikles leads Athens through its Golden Era
449–432	Construction of the Parthenon, a temple dedicated to Athena
430	Just after the Second Peloponesian War begins, a plague erupts in Athens.
429	Perikles dies
404	After the Peloponnesian War, Athens surrenders to Sparta
399	Trial and execution of Socrates
338	Macedonian army defeats Athens and its allies at Khaeronea
336	Alexander the Great becomes king of Macedonia
323	Alexander the Great dies; the Hellenistic period begins
146	The Roman Empire conquers Greece

CHAPTER NOTES

Introduction

1. Robert Garland, *Daily Life of the Ancient Greeks* (Westport, Connecticut: Greenwood Press, 1998), p. 172.
2. H.D. Amos and A.G.P. Lang, *These Were the Greeks* (Chester Springs, Pennsylvania: Dufour Editions, Inc., 1982), p. 65.

Chapter One. Athens, Greatest of the Greek City-States

1. Robert Garland, *Daily Life of the Ancient Greeks* (Westport, Connecticut: Greenwood Press, 1998), p. xx.
2. Lesley Adkins and Roy A. Adkins, *Handbook to Life in Ancient Greece* (New York: Facts On File, Inc., 1997) p. 7.

3. H.D. Amos and A.G.P. Lang, *These Were the Greeks* (Chester Springs, Pennsylvania: Dufour Editions, Inc., 1982) p. 4.
4. Garland, p. 24.
5. Ibid., p. 45.
6. Horizon Magazine, *The Horizon Book of Ancient Greece* (New York: American Heritage Publishing Co., 1965), p. 121.
7. Ibid., p. 163.
8. Garland, p. 149.
9. Ibid., p. 150.

Chapter Two. Women in Greek Society

1. Sarah B. Pomeroy, Stanley M. Burstein, Walter Dolan, & Jennifer Roberts,

Ancient Greece (New York: Oxford University Press, 1999), p. 67.
2. Robert Garland, *Daily Life of the Ancient Greeks* (Westport, Connecticut: Greenwood Press, 1998), p. 48.
3. Ibid.
4. Ibid., p. 51.
5. Zofia Archibald, *Discovering the World of the Ancient Greeks* (New York: Facts on File, 1991), p. 136
6. Garland, p. 110.
7. Horizon Magazine, *The Horizon Book of Ancient Greece* (New York: American Heritage Publishing Co., 1965), p. 260.
8. Pomeroy, et al., p. 141.
9. Joan Breton Connelly, *Portrait of a Priestess* (Princeton, New Jersey: Princeton University Press, 2007), p. 39.
10. Ibid., p. 39.
11. Pomeroy, et al., p. 63.
12. Garland, p. 70.
13. Ibid.

Chapter Three. Children and the Elderly
1. Robert Garland, *Daily Life of the Ancient Greeks* (Westport, Connecticut: Greenwood Press, 1998), p. 57.
2. Ibid.
3. Sarah B. Pomeroy, Stanley M. Burstein, Walter Dolan, & Jennifer Roberts, *Ancient Greece* (New York: Oxford University Press, 1999), p. 130.
4. Garland, p. 60.
5. H.D. Amos and A.G.P. Lang, *These Were the Greeks* (Chester Springs, Pennsylvania: Dufour Editions, Inc., 1982), p. 51.
6. Pomeroy, et al., p. 140.

Chapter Four. In the Home
1. Horizon Magazine, *The Horizon Book of Ancient Greece* (New York: American Heritage Publishing Co., 1965), p. 260.

2. Robert Garland, *Daily Life of the Ancient Greeks* (Westport, Connecticut: Greenwood Press, 1998), p. 84.
3. John Boardman, Jasper Griffin, and Oswyn Murray, *Greece and the Hellenistic World* (Oxford, Great Britain: Oxford University Press, 1988), p. 210.
4. Majorie Quennell and C.H.B. Quennell, *Everyday Things in Ancient Greece* (New York: G.P. Putnam's Sons, 1954), p. 125.
5. Horizon Magazine, p. 261.
6. Garland, p. 88.
7. Ibid., p. 91.

Chapter Five. Outside the Home
1. Sarah B. Pomeroy, Stanley M. Burstein, Walter Dolan, & Jennifer Roberts, *Ancient Greece* (New York: Oxford University Press, 1999), p. 65.
2. H.D. Amos and A.G.P. Lang, *These Were the Greeks* (Chester Springs, Pennsylvania: Dufour Editions, Inc., 1982), p. 71.
3. Majorie Quennell and C.H.B. Quennell, *Everyday Things in Ancient Greece.* (New York: G.P. Putnam's Sons, 1954), p. 110.
4. Edith Hamilton, *Mythology* (New York: New American Library, 1940), p. 16.
5. Robert Garland, *Daily Life of the Ancient Greeks* (Westport, Connecticut: Greenwood Press, 1998), p. 171.
6. Horizon Magazine, *The Horizon Book of Ancient Greece.* (New York: American Heritage Publishing Co., 1965), p. 156.
7. Garland, p. 182.
8. Horizon Magazine, p. 279.
9. Pomeroy, et al., p. 4.
10. Garland, p. 154.
11. Ibid.

FURTHER READING

Books

Ford, Michael. *You Wouldn't Want to Be a Greek Athlete! Races You'd Rather Not Run.* Danbury, Connecticut: Franklin Watts, 2004.

Green, Jen. *Myths of Ancient Greece.* Austin, Texas: Raintree Steck-Vaughn, 2001.

Houle, Michelle M. *Gods and Goddess in Greek Mythology.* Berkeley Heights, New Jersey: Enslow Publishers, 2001.

McCarty, Nick. *The Iliad.* Boston, Massachusetts: Kingfisher, 2004.

McGee, Marni. *Ancient Greece: Archaeology Unlocks the Secrets of Greece's Past.* Washington, D.C.: National Geographic, 2007.

Tracy, Kathleen. *The Life and Times of Homer.* Hockessin, Delaware: Mitchell Lane Publishers, 2005.

Weber, Belinda. *The Best Book of Ancient Greece.* New York: Kingfisher, 2005.

Works Consulted

Adkins, Lesley, and Roy A. Adkins. *Handbook to Life in Ancient Greece.* New York: Facts On File, Inc., 1997.

Amos, H.D., and A.G.P. Lang. *These Were the Greeks.* Chester Springs, Pennsylvania: Dufour Editions, Inc., 1982.

Archibald, Zofia. *Discovering the World of the Ancient Greeks.* New York: Facts on File, 1991.

Boardman, John, Jasper Griffin, and Oswyn Murray. *Greece and the Hellenistic World.* Oxford, Great Britain: Oxford University Press, 1988.

Cartledge, Paul. *The Greeks.* New York: TV Books, 2000.

Connelly, Joan Breton. *Portrait of a Priestess.* Princeton, New Jersey: Princeton University Press, 2007.

Garland, Robert. *Daily Life of the Ancient Greeks.* Westport, Connecticut: Greenwood Press, 1998.

Hamilton, Edith. *Mythology.* New York: New American Library, 1940.

Horizon Magazine. *The Horizon Book of Ancient Greece.* New York: American Heritage Publishing Co., 1965.

Maurice, Frederick. *"The Campaign of Marathon."* The Journal of Hellenic Studies, Vol. 52, Part 1 (1932), pp. 13–24. Published by The Society for the Promotion of Hellenic Studies.

Pomeroy, Sarah B., Stanley M. Burstein, Walter Dolan, & Jennifer Roberts. *Ancient Greece.* New York: Oxford University Press, 1999.

Porter, Eliot. *The Greek World.* New York: E.P. Dutton, 1980.

Quennell, Marjorie, and C.H.B. Quennell. *Everyday Things in Ancient Greece.* New York: G.P. Putnam's Sons, 1954.

On the Internet
Ancient Greece
   http://www.historylink101.com/ancient_greece.htm
Ancient Greece—History, Mythology, Art, War, Culture, Society, and
   Architecture
   http://www.ancientgreece.com/s/Main_Page
Ancient Greece for Kids
   http://greece.mrdonn.org/
Ancient Greece for Kids
   http://www.historyforkids.org/learn/greeks/
Ancient Greece.org
   http://ancient-greece.org/
The Hoplite
   http://www.militaryfactory.com/ancient-warfare/spartan-hoplite.asp

Glossary

affluent (ah-FLOO-ent)—Prosperous.

cloven (KLOH-van)—Split.

defendant (dee-FEN-dunt)—The person who has to defend himself from a claim or suit in court.

deformity (dee-FOR-mih-tee)—A disfigured feature.

loom (LOOM)—A machine for weaving yarn or thread into fabric.

magistrate (MAA-jeh-strayt)—A civil judge.

metaphor (MEH-tuh-for)—A comparison between two dissimilar things, used to make a point.

pitch—Tarlike substance used for filling cracks.

plaintiff (PLAYN-tif)—A person who brings suit in a court.

subordinate (sub-OR-dih-nayt)—To make secondary.

symposium (sim-POH-zee-um)—A dinner party at which men drink, dine, converse, and play games; the plural is *symposia* (sim-POH-zee-uh).

INDEX

ABOUT THE AUTHOR

Russell Roberts has written over 40 books for adults and children on a variety of subjects, including baseball, memory power, business, history, and travel. He has written numerous books for Mitchell Lane Publishers, including Nathaniel Hawthorne, Holidays and Celebrations in Colonial America, What's So Great About Daniel Boone?, Poseidon, The Life and Times of Nostradamus, and How'd They Do That in Elizabethan England? He lives in Bordentown, New Jersey, with his family and a fat, fuzzy, crafty calico cat named Rusti.